AF292180

CONTENTS

INTRODUCTION

Many people love eating sandwiches, especially in the mornings. The Hamilton Beach Dual Breakfast Sandwich Maker has come to change and make things easier in terms of you prepare your sandwiches. With this cooking appliance, you can make two sandwiches and thereby save your precious time.

This book contains sandwich recipes and also more information about the Hamilton Beach Dual Breakfast Sandwich Maker. The recipes in this book are divided in different categories for easy reading.

Happy sandwiching!

CHAPTER 1: FUNDAMENTALS OF HAMILTON BEACH BREAKFAST SANDWICH MAKER

What Is It?

It is a sandwich make that has revolutionized how sandwiches are made because it makes the cooking easier.

The Benefits of Using It

Makes two Sandwiches

The Hamilton Beach Dual Breakfast Sandwich Maker can make two sandwiches at a time. This is something that makes it stand out from the rest of sandwich makers in the market. This saves you time.

Total Control

The Hamilton Beach Dual Breakfast Sandwich Maker gives control of what you are making. You can use your own fresh ingredients unlike those made in stores, drive-thrus and restaurants.

Healthy choices

This sandwich maker gives you options of making healthy sandwiches such as vegetarian, vegan lean meat, whole-grain foods and many other options.

Easy Way to Make Breakfast Sandwiches

Ever imagined a sandwich maker that makes your work easier? The Hamilton Beach Dual Breakfast Sandwich Maker is that device! It can make your sandwich in just five minutes and it is also easy to clean making things generally easy for you.

Easy Clean-up

The Hamilton Beach Dual Breakfast Sandwich Maker is such an easy appliance to clean up unlike many other in the market. You will get to know more about cleaning it in "How to Clean and maintain it".

Unlimited Taste Combinations

A combination of versatility and fresh ingredients makes the Hamilton Beach Dual Breakfast Sandwich Maker the ideal solution for all people. You can personalize each sandwich to the mood of a kid, adult, mood or day of the week.

The Step-by-Step Procedure of Using It

The steps for using the Hamilton Beach Dual Breakfast Sandwich Maker are as follows:

1. Plug the power cord to a power source. A red light will glow.
2. Spray a non-stick cooking spray on the rings as it preheats.
3. Ensure it is closed and the plate for cooking is between the rings.
4. Once preheated, a green light will glow. It goes on and off just like the oven.
5. Use the handles to lift the cover and also lift the ting on top and the cooking plate.
6. Assemble your sandwich
7. Place the bottom half of your bun on the plate at the bottom. Put the ingredients you prefer on top.
8. Move the ring and lower the cooking plate.
9. Beat an egg on the plate.
10. Put the other half of the bun.
11. Cover the lid and cook for up to 10 minutes.
12. Revolve the cooking plate clockwise once cooking is done.
13. Remove the ring and hold the bottom handle to cover using mittens.
14. Use a silicone, wooden or plastic spatula to move the sandwich to a plate. Avoid using utensils that are metallic.
15. Unplug from the power and allow it to cool.

Great Tips for Best Effect

1. For the best results, use buns, breads and bagels.
2. Never smoosh. Lower the lid slowly without pressing it.
3. Timing is key. You need to have a timer to cook for the ideal time.
4. You can have a peek to be sure if it is ready.
5. When covering, use mittens at all times.

How to Clean and Maintain It

To clean this sandwich maker, you need to have unplugged it from the power source and let it cool. Use a wooden or plastic utensil to scrap any ingredients that are bake-on.

Open by holding the bottom handle, lift it straight up to remove the ring assembly to clean inside or in the dishwasher by hand. Spray the cooking plate and rings with a non-stick spray before and after washing for easier cleaning.

Troubleshooting

Below are some ways you fix some issues that may come up while using the Hamilton Beach Dual Breakfast Sandwich Maker.

Ingredients sticking to the cooking plates or rings

Always grease with a non-stick spray prior to preparing your recipe.

The Bread is Overly Browned

To avoid this, cook the eggs alone for a few minutes and then add the bread.

Slow or Low Heating

It takes 5-7 minutes to get the right temperature after which a green light will glow. Low heating means the unit is filled in excess and you should reduce them.

Bread not crispy and eggs under cooked

Different sizes of the same ingredients take different times to cook. A large egg will take more time than a small egg. Frozen ingredients will need an additional minute to be done.

Eggs leaking out

This would mean that you have overfilled the unit and you need to reduce the ingredients. Avoid pressing the cover down too.

Cover rising when cooking

When cooking a large scrambled egg and you whisk it, the cover may rise. Do not press it down but instead leave it that way.

CHAPTER 2: NORMAL BREAKFAST SANDWICHES AND OMELETS

Traditional BLT

Prep Time: 5 minutes/ Cook Time: 5 minutes/ Servings: 1

Ingredients:

- 2 slices white bread
- 3 slices bacon, cooked
- 2 thin slices tomato
- 1 leaf Romaine lettuce, torn in half
- 2 teaspoons mayonnaise

Directions:

1. Spread one teaspoon of mayonnaise on each slice of bread.
2. Preheat the sandwich maker.
3. Place one slice of bread inside the bottom tray of the sandwich maker, mayonnaise-side facing up.
4. Break the slices of bacon in half and place them on top of the bread. Top with the slices of tomato.
5. Top the sandwich with the other slice of bread, mayonnaise-side down.
6. Close the sandwich maker and cook for 4 to 5 minutes.
7. Carefully open the sandwich maker and remove the top slice of bread.
8. Add the lettuce then replace the bread and enjoy your sandwich.

Cheese and Egg Sandwich

Prep Time/Cook Time: 45 Minutes/Serves: 12 Sandwiches

Ingredients:

- English Muffins
- Large eggs
- 10 Ounces cheese, grated
- Butter, or olive oil (optional)

Directions:

1. Lightly oil a muffin tin and crack an egg in each tin.
2. Bake the muffin tin with eggs in a 350°F oven for 10-15 minutes. Depending on your egg size, start checking them early to make sure they are cooked through. Try not to overcook them!
3. Slice all the muffins and toast them in the oven for 10 minutes or you can toast them one at a time if you like.
4. Add an egg, cheese, and any protein or veggies that you want to each sandwich.
5. If you want to eat one right away, stick it in the oven as a sandwich for about 9 minutes to melt the cheese and everything.

Spinach, Parmesan and Egg White

Prep Time: 5 minutes/ Cook Time: 5 minutes/ Serves 1

Ingredients:

- 1 toasted English muffin, sliced
- ½ cup baby spinach leaves
- 2 large egg whites
- 1 tablespoon grated parmesan cheese
- 1 clove garlic, minced

Directions:

1. Preheat the breakfast sandwich maker.
2. Place half of the English muffin, cut-side up, inside the bottom tray of the sandwich maker.
3. Arrange the baby spinach leaves on top of the English muffin.
4. Beat the egg whites, parmesan cheese and garlic in a small bowl.
5. Slide the egg tray into place and pour the egg mixture into it.
6. Top the egg with the other half of the English muffin.
7. Close the sandwich maker and cook for 4 to 5 minutes until the egg is cooked through.
8. Carefully rotate the egg tray out of the sandwich maker then open the sandwich maker and enjoy your sandwich.

Mediterranean Sandwiches

Prep Time 6 minutes/Cook Time: 20 minutes Servings: 4

Ingredients:

- 4 multigrain sandwich thins
- 4 teaspoons olive oil
- 1 tablespoon snipped fresh rosemary
- 4 eggs
- 2 cups fresh baby spinach leaves
- 1 tomato, cut into 8 thin slices
- 4 tablespoons low-fat feta cheese
- ⅛ teaspoon kosher salt
- Freshly ground black pepper.

Directions:

1. Preheat oven to 375°F. Split sandwich thins; brush cut sides with 2 teaspoons of the olive oil. Place on the baking sheet; toast in oven about 5 minutes or until edges are light brown and crisp.

2. In the meantime, in a large skillet heat the remaining 2 teaspoons of olive oil and rosemary over medium-high heat.

3. Break eggs, one at a time, into a skillet. Cook for about 1 minute. Break the yolks with spatula. Flip eggs; cook on other side until done. Remove from heat.

4. Place the bottom halves of the toasted sandwich thins on four serving plates. Divide spinach among sandwich thins on plates. Top each with two of the tomato slice, an egg and 1 tablespoon of the feta cheese. Drizzle with salt and pepper. Top with the remaining sandwich thin halves.

Breakfast Hamburger

Prep time: 10 minutes/Cook Time: 35 minutes/ Servings 4

Ingredients:

Hamburger Pattie

- 2 lb minced beef, 20%+ fat (Note 1)
- Salt and pepper
- 3 onions, sliced into rings
- 2 tbsp oil
- 4 slices cheese (optional)

Hamburger

- 4 soft hamburger buns, lightly toasted
- Lettuce, tomato slices
- Ketchup, mustard, relish, sliced pickles

Directions

1. Separate beef into 4 equal portions. Form patties the size of your buns.
2. Season generously with salt and pepper on both sides. Make a dent on one side (stop burger from becoming dome shaped and shrinking when cooking).
3. Heat 1 tbsp oil in a skillet over high heat. Add onion and cook until wilted and caramelized. Season with salt and pepper, and then remove.
4. Heat 1 tbsp oil until smoking. Add patties and cook for 2 minutes until deep golden with a great crust. Do not press! Turn and cook for 1 minute then top with cheese (if using). Cover with lid and cook for 1 more minute until cheese melts.
5. Meanwhile, lightly toast the cut side of the buns.
6. To serve: Spread base of buns with sauce, condiment of choice. Top with lettuce then tomato, then hamburger patty. Pile over onions, sliced pickles, then more sauce/condiments. Top with lid of bun. Serve immediately.

Classic Egg, Ham and Cheese

Prep Time: 5 minutes/Cook Time: 5 minutes/ Servings: 1

Ingredients:

- 1 toasted English muffin, sliced
- 2 slices deli ham
- 1 slice cheddar cheese
- 1 large egg

Directions:

1. Preheat the sandwich maker.
2. Place half of the English muffin, cut-side up, inside the bottom tray of the sandwich maker.
3. Fold the slices of ham on top of the English muffin half and top with the slice of cheddar cheese.
4. Slide the egg tray into place and crack the egg into it.
5. Top the egg with the other half of the English muffin.
6. Close the sandwich maker and cook for 4 to 5 minutes until the egg is cooked through.
7. Carefully rotate the egg tray out of the sandwich maker then open the sandwich maker and enjoy your sandwich.

Waffle, Egg and Sausage

Prep Time: 5 minutes/ Cook Time: 5 minutes/ Servings: 1

Ingredients:

- 2 round frozen waffles
- 1 pork sausage patty, cooked
- 1 large egg
- 1 teaspoon maple syrup

Directions:

1. Preheat the breakfast sandwich maker.
2. Place one of the waffles inside the bottom tray of the sandwich maker.
3. Put the sausage patty on top of the waffle.
4. Slide the egg tray into place and crack the egg into it.
5. Top the egg with the other waffle.
6. Close the sandwich maker and cook for 4 to 5 minutes until the egg is cooked through.
7. Carefully rotate the egg tray out of the sandwich maker then open the sandwich maker.
8. Remove the top waffle and drizzle the egg with maple syrup.
9. Replace the waffle and enjoy your sandwich.

Sausage and Cheese

Prep Time: 5 minutes/ Cook Time: 5 minutes/ Servings: 1

Ingredients:

- 1 buttermilk biscuit, sliced
- 1 maple pork sausage patty, cooked
- 1 slice cheddar cheese
- 1 large egg, beaten

Directions:

1. Preheat the sandwich maker.
2. Place half of the biscuit, cut-side up, inside the bottom tray of the sandwich maker.
3. Arrange the sausage patty on top of the biscuit and top with the slice of cheddar cheese.
4. Slide the egg tray into place and pour the beaten egg into it.
5. Top the egg with the other half of the biscuit.
6. Close the sandwich maker and cook for 4 to 5 minutes until the egg is cooked through.
7. Carefully rotate the egg tray out of the sandwich maker then open the sandwich maker and enjoy your sandwich.

French Toast Sandwich

Prep Time: 6 Minutes/Cook Time: 10 Minutes/Servings: 2

Ingredients:

- 2 beaten eggs
- ¼ cup milk
- ½ tsp. cinnamon
- Dash of nutmeg
- 2 tbsp. butter
- 4 slices white or sourdough bread
- 4 slices bacon
- 2 eggs
- 4 tbsp. maple syrup

Directions:

1. Combine the eggs, milk, cinnamon and nutmeg in a bowl.
2. Coat each bread slice with the mixture.
3. Heat the butter in the skillet.
4. Fry each slice under they are golden brown. Set aside.
5. Fry the bacon in a skillet. Set aside
6. Fry the eggs (in some of the bacon fat is fine).
7. Lay out two of the French toast slices
8. Top with 2 bacon strips and 1 egg.
9. Drizzle some maple syrup over each toast slice.
10. Top the toast slices with the remaining 2 slices to create a sandwich.

Scrambled Egg and Easy Ham Sandwich

Prep Time: 5 minutes/ Cook Time: 5 minutes/ Serves 1

Ingredients:

- 2 slices whole grain bread
- 2 slices deli ham
- 1 slice Swiss cheese
- 1 large egg
- 2 teaspoons heavy cream
- 1 teaspoon chopped chives

Directions:

1. Preheat the sandwich maker.
2. Place one slice of bread in the bottom tray of the sandwich maker.
3. Arrange the slices of ham on top of the bread and top with the slice of Swiss cheese.
4. Beat together the egg, heavy cream and chives in a small bowl.
5. Slide the egg tray into place over the cheese and pour the beaten egg mixture into the tray.
6. Top the egg mixture with the remaining slice of bread.
7. Close the sandwich maker and cook for 4 to 5 minutes until the egg is cooked through.
8. Carefully rotate the egg tray out of the sandwich maker then open the sandwich maker and enjoy your sandwich.

Avocado, Swiss and Bacon

Prep Time: 5 minutes/ Cook Time: 5 minutes/ Serves 1

Ingredients:

- 1 croissant, sliced
- 2 slices bacon, cooked
- 1 slice Swiss cheese
- ¼ avocado, pitted and sliced
- 1 large egg
- 1 tablespoon basil pesto

Directions:

1. Divide the pesto between the two halves of the croissant, spreading it evenly.
2. Preheat the breakfast sandwich maker.
3. Place half of the croissant, pesto-side up, inside the bottom tray of the sandwich maker.
4. Arrange the slices of bacon on top of the bagel and top with the slice of Swiss cheese.
5. Slide the egg tray into place and crack the egg into it.
6. Top the egg with the other half of the croissant, pesto-side down.
7. Close the sandwich maker and cook for 4 to 5 minutes until the egg is cooked through.
8. Carefully rotate the egg tray out of the sandwich maker then open the sandwich maker and enjoy your sandwich.

CHAPTER 3: RED MEAT BREAKFAST SANDWICHES AND BURGERS 10

Roast Beef Sandwiches

Prep Time: 15 minutes/ Cook Time:1 hour 5 minutes/ Servings: 6

Ingredients:

- 1 red onion, sliced thinly
- 1 tablespoon, plus 2 teaspoons salt
- 6 tablespoons red wine vinegar
- ¾ cupmayonnaise
- ¾ cup sour cream
- ¼ cup plus 2 tablespoons jarred grated horseradish (with liquid)
- 1/2 teaspoon grated lemon zest
- Freshly ground black pepper
- Hot sauce
- 6 Kaiser rolls
- 12 slices ripened tomatoes
- 24 ounces freshly sliced rare roast beef
- 3 cups watercress or arugula

Directions:

1.   In a small bowl, mix onion and 1 tablespoon salt. Set aside for 20 minutes. Rinse the onions with cold running water. Drain and squeeze to remove excess liquid. Combine the onions and the vinegar and marinate at least 30 minutes or up to 24 hours.

2.   In a small bowl, mix together the mayonnaise, sour cream, horseradish, zest, and 2 teaspoon salt. Season generously with pepper and hot sauce to taste. Refrigerate the horseradish sauce for at least 30 minutes.

3.   Preheat the sandwich maker. Slice the rolls in half lengthwise. Shallowly scoop out the inside of each half using your hands. Transfer

the rolls to a baking sheet and arrange scooped-side up. Toast the rolls under the broiler for about 1 minute. Slather the inside of the rolls with the horseradish sauce. On each of the roll bottoms, layer 2 tomato slices and season with salt and pepper to taste.

4.   Top the tomatoes with some of the roast beef overlapped into "ruffles" and season with pepper and salt. Top meat with some of the onions and watercress and cover with the tops of the roll.

5.   Serve and enjoy.

Corned Beef and Sauerkraut Sandwich

Prep Time/Cook Time: 15 Minutes, Serves: 2

Ingredients:

- 8 slices rye bread
- 2 tablespoons butter
- 8 slices cheese
- 1 cup drained sauerkraut
- 8 slices deli sliced corned beef
- ½ cup dressing

Directions:

1. Coat one side of your bread with butter. Then coat the opposite side with dressing.
2. Place the following on four pieces of bread: 1 piece of Swiss, one fourth cup sauerkraut, 2 pieces of corned beef, the rest of the Swiss.
3. Add another piece of bread and make sure the buttered sides are facing outwards.
4. Fry the sandwiches for 15 minutes on each side.

Bacon Hawaiian Sandwich

Prep Time/Cook Time: 15 Minutes, Serves: 4

Ingredients

- 16 slices bacon
- 8 slices toasted white bread
- 20 oz. sliced pineapple, drained
- 8 slices Cheddar cheese

Directions

1. Fry your bacon until crispy then remove any excess oils.
2. Layer your bread in a broiler pan or on a baking sheet.
3. Top the bread with some pineapple, bacon, and cheese.
4. Now broil everything for a few minutes until it is bubbly.
5. Form 4 sandwiches from the toasted bread.

Pork Rib Sandwich

Prep Time/Cook Time: 35 Minutes, Serves: 2

Ingredients

- 14 oz. beef broth
- 3 lbs. boneless pork ribs
- 18 oz. bottle barbeque sauce

Directions

1. Add pork and beef broth into the crock pot.
2. For 4 hours let the pork cook on High. After the cooking time has elapsed break up the pork with a large fork.
3. Set your oven to 350°F before doing anything else.
4. Put your pork in a casserole dish or a large pot then add in your BBQ sauce and cook everything in the oven for 35 minutes.
5. Enjoy with your favorite bread.

The Rustic Beef Sandwich

Prep Time/Cook Time: 21 Minutes, Serves: 4

Ingredients:

- 1 lb. loaf French or Italian-style bread
- ¼ cup minced green onions
- 1 tbsp. milk
- 1/8 tsp. garlic powder
- 1 green bell pepper, sliced in rings
- 1 lb. ground beef
- 1 cup sour cream
- 1 tsp Worcestershire sauce
- ¾ tsp. salt
- 2 tbsps. butter, softened
- 2 tomatoes, sliced
- 1 cup shredded Cheddar cheese

Directions

1. Divide your bread in half, cover it in foil, and place it in the oven at 375 °F for 13 minutes.
2. Fry your beef and onions and remove any excess oils.
3. Now add in the following to the mix: pepper, milk, salt, garlic, Worcestershire, garlic, and sour cream.
4. Heat this mixture for 2 minutes.
5. Coat your bread with butter, then layer the following: half of your beef mix, bell peppers, tomatoes and cheese.
6. Cook everything in the oven for 6 minutes at 350 °F / 180°C.
7. Form a sandwich and enjoy.

Beef and Mushroom Sandwich

Prep Time/Cook Time: 13 Minutes, Serves: 2

Ingredients

- 1 loaf hearty country bread, unsliced
- 3 tbsps. vegetable oil, divided
- 3 lb. boneless beef round steak, 2 inches / 5 cm thick
- 1 onion, thinly sliced
- 2 cup sliced fresh mushrooms
- 1 clove garlic, minced, or to taste
- Salt to taste
- Ground black pepper to taste
- Garlic salt to taste

Directions

1. Slice off a piece of bread from the loaf and keep it for later.
2. Now remove the inside center of the loaf.
3. This space is to be filled later.
4. Fry your steak in 1 tablespoon of veggie oil for 6 minutes per side then place the steak to the side.
5. Stir fry your mushrooms, onions, and garlic for 7 minutes until the onions are see through in 2 more tablespoons of veggie oil.
6. Fill the hollowed bread with: the mushrooms, onions, and steak.
7. Put the first piece of bread you sliced off earlier back on the loaf.
8. Now cover everything with foil.
9. Lay the bread in a casserole dish and place something heavy on top of it. Like a cast iron frying pan with jars of water in it.
10. For 7 hours let the bread sit in the fridge with the pan on top of it.
11. When ready to serve, cut the sandwich into servings.
12. Enjoy.

Deli Corned Beef Slaw Sandwiches

Prep Time/Cook Time: 15 Minutes, Serves: 3

Ingredients:

- 8 slices rye bread
- 1½ cup deli coleslaw
- 10 oz. deli corned beef (thinly sliced)
- 5 slices deli Swiss cheese
- 1/3 cup salad dressing

Directions:

1. Position 4 slices of bread on flat surface.
2. Then, divide coleslaw, corned beef & cheese among them.
3. Next, sprinkle dressing onto all & top with other bread slices.
4. Slice in half & serve.

Gourmet Pork Sandwich

Prep Time/Cook Time: 7 Minutes, Serves: 3

Ingredients

- Choice of greens
- 3 tablespoons mayonnaise
- 1/8 piece red bell pepper,sliced
- 2 sliced Gardenia loaf bread
- 4 lbs. pork strips

Directions

1. Cook pork strips and bell peppers.
2. Coat bread with mayo, stuff with greens, pepper and pork, cover with other bread, and serve.

Beef Broiled Sandwich

Prep Time/Cook Time: 15 Minutes, Serves: 2

Ingredients

- 1 cup chopped cooked beef
- 2 stalks celery, chopped
- 1 carrot, diced
- ¼ cup chopped onion
- 3 tbsps mayonnaise
- ¼ tsp salt
- 1/8 tsp ground black pepper
- 1/8 tsp garlic powder
- 2 sesame seed buns, toasted until the broiler

Directions

1. Get a bowl, combine: garlic powder, beef, black pepper, celery, salt, carrot, mayo, and onion. Stir the mix until it is even.
2. Enjoy on toasted sesame seed buns.

Easy Ginger Beef Sandwiches

Prep Time/Cook Time: 15 Minutes, Serves: 6

Ingredients:

- 1 tbsp. vegetable oil
- 1 1/2 lb. boneless beef sirloin steak (sliced into thin strips)
- 1 onion (sliced)
- 3 garlic cloves (minced)
- 3 large celery ribs (diagonally, thinly sliced)
- 3 tbsp. minced fresh ginger root
- 2 tbsp. soy sauce
- 1 tsp. chili oil
- 6 hoagie rolls (split laterally)

Directions:

1. In a large skillet; heat vegetable oil on medium-high heat.
2. Then, stir in sirloin strips & sauté a few minutes until the strips starts to brown.
3. Next, stir in onion & garlic; sauté for about 2 minutes.
4. Add in the celery & ginger, keep on cooking for about 3 minutes or until the onion has softened.
5. Now, season it with soy sauce & chili oil.
6. Finally, divide among hoagie rolls & serve.

Roast Beef and Provolone Sandwich

Prep Time/Cook Time: 15 Minutes, Serves: 2

Ingredients

- 1 (10.5 oz.) can beef consommé
- 1 cup water
- 1 lb. thinly sliced deli roast beef
- 8 slices provolone cheese
- 4 hoagie rolls, split lengthwise

Directions

1. Set your oven to 350 °F / 350°C before doing anything else.
2. Open your rolls and place them in a casserole dish.
3. Now combine water and beef consommé in a pan to make a broth.
4. Cook your beef in this mixture for 5 minutes.
5. Then divide the meat between your rolls and top them with cheese.
6. Cook the rolls in the oven for 6 minutes.
7. Enjoy the sandwiches dipped in broth.

Buffalo Chicken Grilled Cheese Sandwich

Prep Time/Cook Time: 5 Minutes, Serves: 1

Ingredients:

- ¼ cup cooked shredded chicken (warm)
- 1 tbsp. hot sauce
- 1/2 tablespoon mayo (optional)
- 1 tbsp. carrot (grated)
- 1 tbsp. celery (sliced)
- 1 tbsp. green or red onion (sliced or diced)
- 1 tbsp. blue cheese (crumbled)
- ½ cup cheddar cheese (grated)
- 2 slices bread
- 1 tbsp. butter

Directions:

1. In a small bowl; add & combine the chicken, hot sauce, mayo, carrot, celery & onion.
2. Butter the outside of each bread slice and sprinkle half of the cheeses on the inside of 1 slice of bread
3. Next, top with the buffalo chicken salad, the remaining cheese & finally the other slice of bread.
4. Take a nonstick pan and heat on medium heat.
5. Now, add in the sandwich & grill for about 2 to 4 minutes per side or until golden brown & the cheese melted.

Gourmet Turkey with Apple Sandwich

Prep Time/Cook Time: 7 Minutes, Serves: 1

Ingredients

- 1 tablespoon apple butter
- ¼ cup arugula
- ½ ounce organic cheddar cheese
- 4 ounces cooked turkey breast filet
- 2 slices whole grain bread or Gluten Free bread
- Cooking spray or coconut oil

Directions:

1. In a medium heat nonstick pan coated with cooking spray, cook the sandwich stuffed with apple butter, half cheese, turkey breast, other half cheese and arugula for 2 minutes.
2. Serve.

Fruity Chicken Sandwiches

Prep Time/Cook Time: 15 Minutes, Serves: 8

Ingredients:

- ½ lb. creamy deli fruit salad
- 1 ½ c. roasted deli chicken (chopped)
- 8 lettuce leaves

Directions:

1. Slice in half 4 pita breads & pocket opened.

2. Then, in a medium bowl, add & combine fruit salad & chopped chicken.

3. Next, line pita breads with the lettuce leaves & spoon chicken mixture into the breads.

4. Place into the oven & cook until heated through.

Apricot Chicken Sandwich

Prep Time/Cook Time: 5 Minutes, Serves: 2

Ingredients

- 1 medium chicken breast
- 1 slice of red onion, rings separated
- 6 fresh sage leaves
- 1 tsp. butter
- 1 tsp. canola oil
- 1 tablespoon mayonnaise
- 1 tablespoon sugar free apricot preserves
- 1/3 cup arugula
- 1 slice provolone cheese, halved

Directions:

1. Blend mayonnaise and apricot preserves. Place aside.
2. Grill the chicken breast with salt and pepper, spraying the grill so the breast does not stick.
3. Cook for 3-4 minutes on both sides over medium heat.
4. When cooked through, remove the chicken breast and slice in half, lengthwise.
5. I a small skillet, warm the butter and oil over mid heat.
6. Fry the sage leaves in the skillet until they crisp up.
7. Remove then and position on a paper towel.
8. Apply the apricot mayo spread on the bottom part of the chicken breast.
9. Next layer on the sage leaves, provolone cheese, red onion and arugula.
10. Set the other half of the chicken breast atop and enjoy.

Turkey corned beef and cabbage sandwich

Prep Time/Cook Time: 5 Minutes, Serves: 2

Ingredients:

- 4 slices whole-wheat bread
- 1 tsp light butter
- 1 small can low-sodium turkey corned beef
- ½ cup cabbage, shredded or chopped

Directions:

1. Lightly pat butter on each sandwich maker pan.
2. Make two sandwiches, spreading the turkey corned beef and topping with cabbage.
3. Cook in sandwich maker for about 3 minutes.
4. Serve hot.

Chicken Hot and Sour Sandwich

Prep Time/Cook Time: 6 Minutes, Serves: 4

Ingredients

- 16 oz. chicken, boiled, shredded
- 2 tablespoons soya sauce
- 3 tablespoons tomato sauce
- ½ cup barbecue sauce
- 1 tablespoon apple cider vinegar
- 4 garlic cloves, minced
- 2 tablespoons oil
- 1 teaspoon chili powder
- ¼ teaspoon black pepper
- 1 teaspoon salt
- 2 tablespoons butter
- 1 egg, whisked
- 6 bread slices

Directions

1. Heat oil in pan and fry garlic until fragrant.
2. Transfer chicken and fry till nicely golden.
3. Now add salt, pepper.
4. Add in soya sauce and stir well to combine.
5. Let to cook on medium flame for 3-4 minutes.
6. Transfer to bowl and set aside.
7. In a large bowl combine, barbecue sauce, tomato sauce, vinegar, lemon juice.
8. Take another bread and spread 2 tablespoons of sauce mixture on both sides.
9. Now take another bread slice and top with 2 tablespoons of sauce and spread well, place chicken mixture and spread evenly.

10.	Place first bread slice on chicken and press a little. Top again with chicken mixture and spread with spoon.
11.	Now take third bread slice and spread sauce mixture on.
12.	Place this slice on sandwich and press a little.
13.	Brush top of sandwich with egg and place into microwave for 20-25 seconds.
14.	Now remove from microwave and flip the side, brush again with egg and place in microwave for 20-25 seconds.
15.	Now place on cutting board and cut triangularly.
16.	Serve with chili garlic sauce and enjoy.
17.	Enjoy.

Grilled Chicken & Apple Sandwiches

Prep Time/Cook Time: 5 Minutes, Serves: 6

Ingredients:

- 2 oz. dark & light meat chicken (drained)
- 1/2 c. mayonnaise
- 1 tbsp. lemon juice
- 1 1/2 c. grated cheese
- 2 stalks celery (chopped)
- 1 apple (finely chopped)
- 1/2 c. grated carrot (if desired)
- 12 slices whole-wheat bread
- 2 tbsps. butter

Directions:

1. Take a small bowl; add & combine the chicken, mayonnaise, lemon juice, cheese, celery, apple & carrot.
2. Then, make the sandwiches with the bread.
3. Spread outside of sandwiches with the butter.
4. Next, grill the sandwiches, covered on medium heat, spinning once, until cheese begins to melt & bread is toasted.
5. You can also cook on dual-contact indoor grill for about 3 to 5 minutes or until bread is golden brown.

Chicken Light Sandwich

Prep Time/Cook Time: 15 Minutes, Serves: 4

Ingredients

- 1 cup chicken, boneless, small pieces
- 1 onion, chopped
- 3 garlic cloves, minced
- 1 cup mayonnaise
- ¼ teaspoon black pepper
- ¼ teaspoon salt
- 2 tablespoon chopped spring onion
- 6 bread slices
- 1 tablespoon butter

Directions

1. Melt butter in pan and fry garlic for about 30 seconds.
2. Transfer chicken in pan and stir fry until cooked or no longer pink.
3. Add in black pepper, salt and mix to combine.
4. Put chicken into bowl and leave to cool.
5. Take a large bowl and mix chicken, mayonnaise, and spring onion.
6. Place 2 bread slice on cutting board and spread 3-4 tablespoons of mixture over individually, top them with two more bread slices and spread remaining chicken mixture, finally place remaining bread slices over and press them a little to make 2 sandwiches.
7. Now cut each sandwich triangularly and then cut each triangle again from center or diagonally.
8. Serve and enjoy.

Baked Turkey Sandwich

Prep Time/Cook Time: 25 Minutes, Serves: 8

Ingredients

- 1 onion (finely chopped)
- 1 tbsp. olive oil
- 1/3 c. butter or mayonnaise
- 2 tbsps. Dijon mustard
- 1 tsp. poppy seed
- 8 rolls (split & slightly hollowed out)
- 1 ½ lbs. thinly sliced turkey
- 8 slices cheese

Directions:

1. Pre-heat the oven up to 350 degrees.
2. In small pan, cook onion with olive oil until tender. Remove & let it cool for about 10 minutes.
3. Next, in a small bowl; add & combine the butter or mayo, mustard, onion mixture & poppy seed; spread it onto cut sides of rolls.
4. Now, fill the rolls with turkey & cheese.
5. Wrap each in aluminum foils; bake for about 15 to 5 minutes or until sandwiches gets hot & cheese is melted.

Gourmet Chicken and Mushroom Sandwich

Prep Time/Cook Time: 12 Minutes, Serves: 4

Ingredients

- Salt and freshly ground black pepper
- juice of 1/2 lemon
- 1 small red onion, diced
- 2 tablespoons butter
- ¼ cup mayonnaise
- ¼ cup of fresh basil leaves, chopped
- ½ cup walnuts, toasted and chopped
- ¾ lbs. mushrooms of your choice
- 1 large avocado, firm but ripe, pitted, peeled and diced
- 2 scallions chopped
- 4 slices of Whole Grain Bread, toasted
- 3 chicken breast halves, about 1 1/2 lb. total, cooked (roasted)

Directions

1. In a medium high heat pan coated with butter, cook mushrooms for 5 to 7minutes, then flavor with pepper and salt.
2. In a mixing bowl, mix mayonnaise, scallions and lemon juice, fold and mix into ¼ inch pieces' chicken cube.
3. Serve with toasted bread.

Light and creamy tuna sandwich

Prep Time/Cook Time: 5 Minutes, Serves: 2

Ingredients:

- 4 slices whole-wheat bread
- ½ tsp olive oil
- ½ cup canned tuna chunks in water
- ½ onion, chopped
- 2 tbsps. light mayonnaise

Directions:

1. Lightly pat olive oil on each sandwich maker pan.
2. Mix together the tuna, light mayonnaise, and onions.
3. Make two sandwiches with the tuna mixture.
4. Cook in sandwich maker for about 3 minutes.
5. Serve hot.

Tuna nicoise salad-wich

Prep Time/Cook Time: 5 Minutes, Serves: 2

Ingredients:

- 4 slices whole-wheat bread
- 1 tsp olive oil
- 1 can tuna chunks in water, drained
- 1 medium egg, hard-boiled, sliced
- ¼ cup tomatoes, diced
- ¼ cup fresh basil leaves
- 2 tbsps. white wine vinegar

Directions:

1. Lightly pat olive oil on each sandwich maker pan.
2. Mix together tuna, tomatoes, olive oil, and white wine vinegar.
3. Make two sandwiches with tuna mixture, egg slices and basil leaves.
4. Cook in sandwich maker for about 3 minutes.
5. Serve hot.

Spanish sardines sandwich

Prep Time/Cook Time: 5 Minutes, Serves: 2

Ingredients:

- 4 slices whole-wheat bread
- 4 pcs canned Spanish sardines in olive oil, drained sliced in halves
- 1 clove garlic, chopped
- 1 tsp. lime juice

Directions:

1. Lightly pat olive oil on each sandwich maker pan.
2. Make two sandwiches with the sardines, sprinkles of garlic and lime juice.
3. Cook in sandwich maker for about 3 minutes.
4. Serve hot.

Salmon and cream cheese grilled sandwich

Prep Time/Cook Time: 5 Minutes, Serves: 2

Ingredients:

- 4 slices whole-wheat bread
- ½ tsp olive oil
- ½ medium salmon fillet, sliced into two layers
- 2 tbsps. light cream cheese
- 1 tsp lime juice
- 1 tsp dried herbs of choice (oregano, basil, rosemary, thyme, etc.)

Directions:

1. Lightly pat olive oil on each sandwich maker pan.
2. Spread cream cheese on one side of each bread.
3. Make two sandwiches with salmon fillet, sprinkles of lime juice and herbs.
4. Cook in sandwich maker for about 3 minutes.
5. Serve hot.

Warm California maki sandwich

Prep Time/Cook Time: 5 Minutes, Serves: 2

Ingredients:

- 4 slices whole-wheat bread
- ½ tsp olive oil
- 4 pcs kani (crab) sticks, sliced
- ½ mango, sliced
- ½ cucumber, thinly sliced
- 2 tbsps. MSG-free Japanese mayo, or light mayonnaise

Directions:

1. Lightly pat olive oil on each sandwich maker pan.
2. Mix together the kani sticks, cucumber, mayonnaise, and mango slices.
3. Make two sandwiches with the kani mixture.
4. Cook in sandwich maker for about 3 minutes.
5. Serve hot.

Gourmet Smoked Salmon with Tarragon Sandwich

Prep Time/Cook Time: 45 Minutes, Serves: 2 Sandwiches

Ingredients

- 6 hard-boiled large eggs, peeled
- 2 teaspoons finely chopped fresh tarragon
- 1 tablespoon finely chopped shallot
- 2 tablespoons drained capers, rinsed and finely chopped
- 1/2 cup mayonnaise
- 6 (4- to 5-inch) soft round seeded rolls, split
- 18 watercress sprigs, tough stems discarded
- ¼ pound sliced smoked salmon

Directions

1. Smash eggs, mix with tarragon, capers, shallot, mayonnaise, pepper and salt.
2. Stuff sandwiches with egg salad, watercress, rolls and salmon.

Tuna and Lettuce Sandwich

Prep Time/Cook Time: 15 Minutes, Serves: 2 Sandwiches

Ingredients

- 12 oz. tuna fillets, pieces
- 1 cup cream cheese
- 3 garlic cloves, minced
- 1 teaspoon ginger powder
- ¼ cup mayonnaise
- ¼ teaspoon salt
- 4 bread slices
- 4 lettuce leaf
- ½ teaspoon white pepper
- ¼ teaspoon salt
- 1 tablespoon olive oil

Directions

1. Heat oil in pan and fry garlic for 1 minute.
2. Transfer tune and stir fry until no longer pink.
3. Add in ginger powder, salt and pepper.
4. Cook for 5-6 minutes and the remove from heat and transfer into bowl.
5. Take folks and shred tuna well.
6. Place lettuce leaves with tune mixture between tow bread slices. Make another sandwich in same way.
7. Serve and enjoy.

Microwave Tuna Sandwiches

Prep Time/Cook Time: 15 Minutes, Serves: 3

Ingredients:

- ¼ lb. cheese (cubed)
- 3 hardboiled eggs (chopped)
- 1 (7 oz.) can tuna
- 2 tbsp. sweet pickle (chopped)
- 1/2 c. miracle whips salad Dressing

Directions:

1. In a bowl, add & combine all the ingredients together.
2. Then, spread it on hamburger buns.
3. Place in microwave and bake on high until cheese is melted.

Wasabi mayo shrimp sandwich

Prep Time/Cook Time: 5 Minutes, Serves: 2

Ingredients:

- 4 slices whole-wheat bread
- ½ tsp olive oil
- 16 pcs medium shrimp, steamed or boiled
- 2 tbsps. MSG-free Japanese mayo, or light mayonnaise
- 1 tsp lime juice
- 1 tsp wasabi powder

Directions:

1. Lightly pat olive oil on each sandwich maker pan.
2. Mix together in a bowl the shrimp, mayonnaise, wasabi powder, and lime juice.
3. Make two sandwiches with the shrimp mixture.
4. Cook in sandwich maker for about 3 minutes.
5. Serve hot.

Hot Seafood Sandwiches

Prep Time/Cook Time: 10 Minutes, Serves: 4

Ingredients:

- 1/2 tsp. dried dill weed
- 2 tbsp. Dijon mustard
- 2 c. deli seafood salad
- 8 slices sourdough bread
- 1 c. cheese (shredded)
- ½ c. cocktail sauce
- 4 tbsps. butter (softened)

Directions:

1. Firstly, stir dill & mustard into seafood salad.
2. Then, divide among half of the bread slices and sprinkle with cheese.
3. Top with cocktail sauce & with remaining bread slices.
4. Next, butter outsides of sandwiches & cook into a skillet or dual contact grill until bread is toasted & crisp.
5. Now, slice in half & serve immediately.

Asian bean sprouts salad-wich

Prep Time/Cook Time: 10 Minutes, Serves: 2

Ingredients:

- 4 slices bread
- 1 tsp sesame oil
- ½ cup bean sprouts, rinsed
- 1 clove garlic, chopped
- 1 tsp onions, chopped
- 2 tbsps. MSG-free soy sauce

Directions:

1. Lightly pat sesame oil on each sandwich maker pan.
2. Mix together the bean sprouts, garlic, onions, soy sauce, and sesame oil.
3. Make two sandwiches with bean sprouts mixture.
4. Cook in sandwich maker for about 5 minutes.
5. Serve hot.

Grilled samosa-wich

Prep Time/Cook Time: 5 Minutes, Serves: 2

Ingredients:

- 4 pcs whole-wheat pita bread
- ½ tsp. olive oil
- ½ cup potato, boiled and mashed
- ¼ cup green peas
- 1 tsp ground spices of choice (cumin, turmeric, chilies, etc.)
- 1 tsp lime juice

Directions:

1. Lightly pat olive oil on each sandwich maker pan.
2. For the filling, mix together potatoes, peas, spices, and lime juice.
3. Make four pita folds with samosa filling.
4. Cook in sandwich maker for about 3 minutes.
5. Serve hot.

Baked beans sandwich grill

Prep Time/Cook Time: 5 Minutes, Serves: 2

Ingredients:

- 4 slices whole-wheat bread
- ½ tsp. light butter
- ½ cup canned low sodium baked beans

Directions:

1. Lightly pat butter on each sandwich maker pan.
2. Place the bread slices on the sandwich maker pan.
3. Spread the baked beans on the bread slices.
4. Top with the remaining bread slices.
5. Cook in sandwich maker for about 3 minutes.
6. Serve hot

Vegan Sausage Sandwich

Prep Time/Cook Time: 10 Minutes, Serves: 1

Ingredients:

- 1 vegan English muffin, sliced
- 1 vegan sausage patty, cooked
- 1 slice Vegan cheese
- 1-ounce firm tofu
- Pinch garlic powder
- Salt and pepper to taste

Directions:

1. Cut the tofu into a circle and sprinkle it with garlic powder, salt and pepper.
2. Heat the oil in a small skillet and add the tofu. Cook for 2 to 3 minutes on each side until lightly browned.
3. Preheat the breakfast sandwich maker.
4. Place half of the English muffin, cut-side up, inside the bottom tray of the sandwich maker.
5. Top the muffin with the sausage patty, vegan cheese and tofu.
6. Place the second half of the English muffin on top of the tofu.
7. Close the sandwich maker and cook for 4 to 5 minutes until heated through.
8. Carefully open the sandwich maker and enjoy your sandwich.

Eggs Florentine Biscuit

Prep Time/Cook Time: 10 Minutes, Serves: 1

Ingredients:

- 1 slice multigrain bread
- 1 large egg
- 2 tbsp. plain nonfat yogurt
- ¼ tsp. Dijon mustard
- ½ cup baby spinach
- 1 tbsp. minced yellow onion
- 1 tsp. olive oil

Directions:

1. Heat the oil in a small skillet over medium heat. Add the onion and spinach and stir well.
2. Cook for 2 minutes, stirring, until the spinach is just wilted. Set aside.
3. Preheat the breakfast sandwich maker.
4. Place the piece of bread inside the bottom tray of the sandwich maker.
5. Whisk together the yogurt and mustard in a small bowl then brush over the piece of bread.
6. Top the bread with the cooked spinach and onion mixture.
7. Slide the egg tray into place and crack the egg into it. Use a fork to stir the egg, just breaking the yolk.
8. Close the sandwich maker and cook for 4 to 5 minutes until the egg is cooked through.
9. Carefully rotate the egg tray out of the sandwich maker then open the sandwich maker and enjoy your sandwich.

Prep Time/Cook Time: 15 Minutes, Serves: 2

Ingredients:

- 2 whole wheat bagels, sliced

4 slices of tomato

4 baby Bella mushrooms, finely sliced

4 eggs

2 vegetarian sausage patties

½ cup of baby spinach leaves, well rinsed

4 tablespoons of skim milk

Directions:

1. Preheat the sandwich maker.

2. Combine the milk and eggs then whisk.

3. Take the bottom half of one of the whole wheat bagels, placing it in the bottom of the sandwich maker.

4. Place 1 vegetarian sausage patty on top. Then, place ½ of the mushrooms and 2 tomato slices on top of the patty.

5. Pour half of the egg mixture onto the egg plate, then placing the top of the whole wheat bagel in the top slot.

6. Cook for five minutes and make sure the eggs are fully cooked.

7. Take the egg plate out of the sandwich maker, then opening it and taking the sandwich out.

8. Remove the top of the bagel, topping with half of the baby spinach leaves. Top with the top of the bagel.

9. Repeat with the remaining bagel.

10. Eat right away to enjoy it while it is warm.

Grilled hummus sandwich

Prep Time/Cook Time: 45 Minutes, Serves: 2

Ingredients:

- 4 pcs whole-wheat pita bread
- ½ tsp olive oil
- 2 tbsps. hummus
- ¼ cup tomatoes, diced
- ¼ cup onions, chopped

Directions:

1. Lightly pat olive oil on each sandwich maker pan.
2. Mix together in a bowl the hummus, onions and tomatoes.
3. Make four pita folds with hummus mixture.
4. Cook in sandwich maker for about 3 minutes.
5. Serve hot.

Vegetarian Omelet Sandwich

Prep Time/Cook Time: 10 Minutes, Serves: 4

Ingredients:

- 4 whole wheat bagels
- 1 cup of red bell pepper, chopped
- 4 green onions, thinly sliced
- 1 cup of chopped red onion
- 1 cup of chopped baby bella mushrooms
- 8 eggs, well beaten
- 1 cup of Havarti cheese, shredded
- 4 tablespoons of sour cream
- Ground pepper and salt to taste

Directions:

1. Begin by making sure that you preheat the sandwich maker before you get started.
2. In a skillet, sauté the bell pepper, green onions, red onion and mushrooms in a bit of olive oil or with a bit of cooking spray. Cook until the veggies are tender. Set aside.
3. In a small bowl, combine the eight eggs, Havarti cheese, salt, pepper and sour cream. Beat until the mixture is combined.
4. Place the bottom of one whole wheat bagel in the bottom slot of the sandwich maker.
5. In the egg slot, place ¼ of the egg mixture. Top with the top of the whole wheat bagel.
6. Cook in the breakfast sandwich maker for about five minutes, ensuring that the eggs cook all the way through.
7. Take out the egg plate and then carefully remove the sandwich from the appliance.
8. Repeat the process with the remaining 3 bagels.
9. Enjoy while hot.

Guacamole sandwich grill

Prep Time/Cook Time: 5 Minutes, Serves: 2

Ingredients:

- 4 pcs whole-wheat pita bread
- ½ tsp olive oil
- ½ cup avocado, mashed
- ¼ cup tomatoes, diced
- ¼ cup onions, chopped
- 1 tsp lime juice

Directions:

1. Lightly pat olive oil on each sandwich maker pan.
2. For the guacamole, mix together the avocado, tomatoes, onions, and lime juice.
3. Make four pita folds with the guacamole.
4. Cook in sandwich maker for about 3 minutes.
5. Serve hot.

Cinnamon Raisin Apple Sandwich

Prep Time/Cook Time: 10 Minutes, Serves: 1

Ingredients:

- 2 slices cinnamon raisin bread
- ½ small apple, sliced thin
- 1 thin slice cheddar cheese
- ½ teaspoon unsalted butter
- 1 Pinch ground cinnamon and nutmeg

Directions:

1. Preheat the breakfast sandwich maker.
2. Place one slice of bread inside the bottom tray of the sandwich maker. Spread the bread with butter.
3. Top the bread with the slices of apple then sprinkle them with cinnamon and nutmeg.
4. Place the slice of cheddar cheese over the apples. Top the cheese with the other piece of bread.
5. Close the sandwich maker and cook for 4 to 5 minutes until it is heated through.
6. Carefully open the sandwich maker and enjoy your sandwich.

Sweet Potato Cakes Burger

Prep Time/Cook Time: 45 Minutes, Serves: 4

Ingredients

- 300 g Orange Sweet Potatoes, grated
- 4 whole eggs
- 100 g buckwheat flour
- 15 g fresh mint, chopped
- Mushroom and red onion mix
- 8 flat button mushroom
- 1 red onion
- Olive oil
- Salt and pepper
- Avocado burger sauce
- 1 avocado
- 1 shallot, finely chopped
- 10 g fresh mint, chopped
- 1 teaspoon lime juice
- Olive oil
- Salt, pepper
- Burger meat-100 g minced beef per burger

Directions:

Sweet Potatoes Cakes:

1. Peel the orange sweet potatoes.
2. Cut the sweet potatoes in cube and also grated them into a food processor.
3. In a dish blend the grated sweet potatoes with buckwheat flour, chopped mint, whole eggs, salt and pepper.
4. Heat 3 tablespoon of olive-oil in a sauce pan.
5. Use a metal cookie cutter press to form the cakes into the sauce pan.

6.	Put the metallic cookie cutter circle shape into the sauce pan and then fill in with the sweet potatoes combination.
7.	Press firmly with the cutter press to compact the cakes.
8.	It is important that you remove all air to produce a firm and compact cake.
9.	Fry for 10 minutes on each side.
10.	Set aside onto absorbent towel to take away the excess of oil.
11.	Mushroom and red onion mix
12.	Cut the red onion and mushrooms.
13.	Heat 1 teaspoon of olive-oil into a sauce pan.
14.	Fry the veggies until soft and tender.
15.	Insert salt and pepper.
16.	Put aside.

Avocado Shallot Sauce:
1.	Strip the Avocado.
2.	Take away the avocado kernel creating an avocado puree by utilizing a fork.
3.	Add 1 teaspoon of lime juice, chopped mint and finely chopped shallot.
4.	Include salt and pepper.

Burger:
1.	Grill the beef patties onto a Barbecue or a sauce pan with a bit of olive-oil.
2.	In a dish place a sweet potato cake.
3.	Spread avocado sauce, include the rocket salad, beef patty, grilled mushroom/red onion, and avocado sauce and also top up with another sweet potato cake.
4.	Eat immediately.
5.	Another option is to include low fat cheese.

Steak Sandwiches

Prep Time/Cook Time: 15 Minutes, Serves: 4 Sandwiches

Ingredients:

- 2 small steaks, sliced
- 1 tsp lemon juice
- 2 tbsps. tarragon
- Salt and pepper to taste
- 4 crusty gluten-free rolls
- Lettuces
- 1 sliced onion

Directions:

1. Grill or broil the steaks and slice.
2. Mix the lemon juice and tarragon.
3. Season the steaks according to taste.
4. Toast the rolls for a few minutes
5. Layer rolls with a piece of lettuce.
6. Divide the sliced meat onto the rolls and drizzle the lemon juice.
7. Top with onion.

Crab Salad Sandwich

Prep Time/Cook Time: 15 Minutes, Serves: 3

Ingredients:

- 2 tbsps. mayonnaise
- 1 tbsp. lemon juice
- ½ cup grated gruyere cheese
- Salt and pepper to taste
- 1 can drained crabmeat.
- 4 thick slices gluten-free bread

Directions:

1. Mix together the mayonnaise, juice, cheese and seasoning.
2. Add the crabmeat and stir well.
3. Spread the crabmeat salad on two bread slices and cover with the other two.
4. Grill on both sides using a skillet.

Turkey Burgers

Prep Time/Cook Time: 45 Minutes, Serves: 12 burgers

Ingredients:

- 1 ½ lbs. ground turkey
- 1 garlic clove - minced
- 2 tbsps. diced parsley
- 2 chopped scallions
- 1 egg white
- 1 tbsp. olive oil
- 1 tsp Worcestershire sauce
- ¼ cup gluten-free bread crumbs
- Salt and pepper to taste
- 12 gluten free buns

Directions:

1. Preheat oven to 350 degrees.
2. Mix all of the ingredients by hand.
3. Shape mixture into 12 patties.
4. Bake for 40 minutes.
5. Place burgers in a bun.
6. Add tomato slices, if desire.

Grilled Cheese

Prep Time/Cook Time: 15 Minutes, Serves: 4 Sandwiches

Ingredients:

- 8 pieces of bread
- 4 tsp mustard
- 8 oz. Swiss cheese – grated
- 8 oz. sliced smoked ham
- 2 tsps. unsalted butter

Directions:

1. Spread half the bread with mustard; the other half with butter.
2. Add the cheese and ham and form sandwiches.
3. Butter the outside of the sandwiches; grill both sides until browned.
4. Serve hot.

Croque Monsieur

Prep Time/Cook Time: 15 Minutes, Serves: 1

Ingredients:

- 1 gluten-free baguette
- 3 tbsps. cream cheese
- 8 slices of thin ham
- 2 slices Swiss cheese

Directions:

1. Heat up the broiler.
2. Cut loaf diagonally in half.
3. Place bread under broiler for a few second.
4. Top with the cream cheese; add the ham and cheese.
5. Place back under broiler until cheese is melted.

Turkey Club

Prep Time/Cook Time: 10 Minutes, Serves: 2 sandwiches

Ingredients:

- 4 slices gluten-free whole wheat bread
- 2 tbsps. mayonnaise
- 2 tsp Dijon mustard
- 1 avocado - sliced
- 4 slices roasted turkey
- 2 pieces, lettuce

Directions:

1. Toast the whole wheat bread slices.
2. Spread mustard and mayonnaise on 2 slices of bread.Top with avocado slices.
3. Place lettuce on bread, add turkey slices.
4. Close sandwich.

Portabella and Halloumi Burger

Prep Time/Cook Time: 15 Minutes, Serves: 2

Ingredients

- 4 portabella mushroom caps with stems removed
- 3 ½ tablespoons balsamic vinegar
- 2 tablespoons olive oil
- 2 thin slices halloumi
- 2 thick slices tomato
- Sea salt and pepper
- 1 handful basil leaves

Directions:

1. Warm grill to medium-high temperature.
2. Wash the mushroom caps and then dry.
3. In a container, blend balsamic vinegar and olive oil.
4. Position the mushrooms gill side down in the mix.
5. Grill the mushrooms on the gill side first for approximately 5 minutes or till they begin to sweat.
6. Flip over, grill 2 to 3 minutes more.
7. Position the halloumi on grill and grill 2 minutes on both sides over fairly high heat.
8. Add salt and pepper onto the tomato.
9. Assemble the "burger", mushroom as the bun, the halloumi cheese as the burger, add mildly salted tomato and crisp basil leaves.
10. Wrap up and serve.

Italian Meatball Sub

Prep Time/Cook Time: 25 Minutes, Serves: 3

Ingredients:

- ½ lb. ground beef and ½ lb. ground pork
- ¾ cup gluten-free bread crumbs
- 1 well-beaten egg
- 2 tsps. oregano
- 2 tbsps. parsley - chopped
- 1 clove minced garlic
- 2 tbsps. Parmesan cheese
- 1 gluten-free baguette
- 1 ½ tbsps. virgin olive oil
- 1/8 tsp salt
- 14 oz. spaghetti sauce
- 4 provolone cheese slices

Directions:

1. Preheat oven to 350 degrees.
2. Mix together the beef and pork.Add in the bread crumbs, egg, oregano, parsley, garlic, and cheese.Blend well.Form 12 meatballs.
3. Bake meatballs for 15 minutes.
4. Meanwhile, cut the baguette lengthwise and brush with oil and sprinkle with salt.
5. Warm up the spaghetti sauce.
6. Place cooked meatballs into the sauce.
7. Spoon the meatballs and sauce onto the toasted baguette.Add the cheese.
8. Bake for 4 more minutes.

Prosciutto and Provolone Sandwich

Prep Time/Cook Time: 15 Minutes, Serves: 2 Sandwiches

Ingredients:

- 4 gluten-free sourdough bread slices
- 4 tbsps. pesto sauce
- 3 oz. prosciutto
- 2 slices provolone

Directions:

1. Cover sourdough slices with pesto sauce.
2. Add prosciutto and provolone to 2 bread slices.
3. Top with remaining 2 slices.

Cherry Chocolate Sandwich

Prep Time/Cook Time: 8 Minutes, Serves: 1

Ingredients:

- 6 Cherry pieces, fresh, de - pitted and sliced
- 1 ½ tbsp. Chocolate spread
- 2 bread pieces
- 1 tsp. Olive oil

Directions:

1. Spread the chocolate on the bread. You can also use a different chocolate spread or a combo.
2. Wash and de – pit the cherries. Slice in half.
3. Layer the cherries over the chocolate and top with the other half of the sandwich. Rub the outer side with olive oil.
4. Press on the sandwich maker for about 2 minutes per side.
5. Cut in half and serve.

Apple cinnamon sandwich

Prep Time/Cook Time: 10 Minutes, Serves: 2

Ingredients:

- 4 slices whole-wheat bread
- ½ tsp. light butter
- ½ apple, sliced
- 1 tsp. ground cinnamon
- 2 tsps. pure maple syrup

Directions:

1. Lightly pat butter on each sandwich maker pan.
2. Spread maple syrup on each bread slice.
3. Make two sandwiches, layering apple slices, and sprinkles of cinnamon powder.
4. Cook in sandwich maker for about 3 minutes.
5. Serve hot.

Nutella Sandwich

Prep Time/Cook Time: 10 Minutes, Serves: 1

Ingredients:

- 1 tbsp. Nutella
- 2 slices of French bread
- 1 tbsp. Marshmallow Cream
- ½ Banana, sliced
- Butter

Directions:

1. Heat the sandwich maker.
2. Spread Nutella on one side of the bread slice and the marshmallow crema on another.
3. Place the banana slices on the marshmallow cream and sandwich both sides together. Batter the outside.
4. Press with the sandwich maker and cook for about 5 minutes.
5. Serve and enjoy!

Caramel Strawberries Sandwich

Prep Time/Cook Time: 10 Minutes, Serves: 4

Ingredients:

- 4 Butter Croissants, large
- 4 tbsp. Caramel Sauce, salted
- 8 sliced Strawberries
- 9 Marshmallows, large, cut into slices
- Cooking spray

Directions:

1. Slice the croissants in half. Spread ½ tbsp. of caramel on each.
2. On one of the sides layer the strawberry slices and on the other layer the marshmallow slices.
3. Bring the sides together to make a sandwich.
4. Preheat the sandwich maker and spray with a cooking spray.
5. Cook the sandwiches for 2 minutes and flip. Cook for 2 more minutes.
6. Remove and let it rest for 1 minute.
7. Cut in half and serve.

Avocado and Chickpea Sandwiches

Prep Time/Cook Time: 7 Minutes, Serves: 4

Ingredients:

- 4 slices white bread
- ½ cup canned chickpeas
- 1 small avocado
- 2 green onions, finely chopped
- 1 egg, hard boiled
- ½ tomato, thinly sliced
- ½ cucumber, thinly sliced
- Salt, to taste

Directions:

1. Mash the avocado and chickpeas with a fork or potato masher until smooth.
2. Add in green onions and salt and combine well.
3. Spread this mixture on the four slices of bread.
4. Top each slice with tomato, cucumber and egg, and serve.

Peanut Butter Bagel Sandwich

Prep Time/Cook Time: 15 Minutes, Serves: 4

Ingredients:

- 4 Bagels, split
- ½ cup Marshmallows, mini
- ¼ cup chunks milk Chocolate
- ¼ cup Peanut butter, creamy
- 4 tbsp. unsalted Butter

Directions:

1. Preheat the sandwich maker on medium heat.
2. On one half spread the peanut butter evenly. Top with marshmallows and chocolate chunks. Top with the other half of the beagles.
3. Butter the sandwich maker and add the sandwiches. Press and cook for 5 minutes, or until the marshmallows and chocolate melt.
4. Let it cool for about 10 minutes.
5. Serve and enjoy!

Apple, Cheddar and Cinnamon-Raisin Sandwich

Prep Time/Cook Time: 10 Minutes, Serves: 1

Ingredients:

- 1 cinnamon raisin bagel
- ½ medium granny smith apple, thinly sliced
- 1 slice of sharp cheddar cheese

Directions:

1. Start by preheating the breakfast sandwich maker.
2. While the appliance is preheating, slice half of an apple very thinly.
3. Slice the bagel as well.
4. Take the bottom of the bagel and place it in the bottom of the sandwich maker.
5. Remove the cooking plate, since you will not need it for this recipe.
6. Top the bottom of the bagel with the thin slices of apple.
7. Place the slice of sharp cheddar on top of the apple slices.
8. Add the top of the bagel to the top slot.
9. Cook for 3-4 minutes, ensuring that the cheese is nicely melted.
10. Open and carefully take the sandwich out.
11. Enjoy immediately.

3 x Sweet Croissant Sandwiches

Prep Time/Cook Time: 20 Minutes, Serves: 3 Sandwiches

Ingredients:

- Banana Almond Croissant
- 1 Croissant, Fresh
- 3 tbsp. Almond Butter, Salted
- 1 Banana
- 1 tbsp. of Brown Sugar
- Nutella Strawberry Croissant
- 1 Croissant, Fresh
- 5 Fresh Strawberries
- 3 tbsp. of Nutella
- 2 tbsp. Walnuts, roasted
- S'mores Croissant
- 1 Croissant, Fresh
- 3 tbsp. Marshmallow, whipped
- 1 piece, Graham Cracker
- 1 bar Dark Chocolate

Directions:

1. Cut the croissants in half.
2. Spread almond butter on both croissants halves. Top with bananas. Sprinkle sugar. Set aside.
3. Spread Nutella on both croissants half and layer sliced strawberries. Sprinkle with roasted walnuts and set aside.
4. Spread whipped marshmallow on both croissants half. Add dark chocolate and top with graham cracker. Set aside.
5. Top them with the second croissants haves and place on the sandwich maker. Cook each for 5 minutes.
6. Serve halved and enjoy!

Raspberry Sandwich

Prep Time/Cook Time: 6 Minutes, Serves: 1

Ingredients:

- 2 slices of Challah bread
- 2 tbsp. of Cream cheese
- ½ tbsp. Butter, melted
- 2 tbsps. Raspberry Preserves

Directions:

1. Turn on medium-high heat and preheat the sandwich maker.
2. Spread the cheese on one of the bread slices.
3. Spread the raspberry on the other bread slices.
4. Sandwich together and brush with butter.
5. Cook for 4 minutes.
6. Cut the sandwich in half and serve.

Banana Foster Sandwich

Prep Time/Cook Time: 10 Minutes, Serves: 8

Ingredients:

- 4 oz. softened Cream Cheese
- 2 tbsp. of Brown sugar
- ½ cup Bananas, chopped
- 2 oz. Chocolate, chopped, Semi-Sweet
- 8 Bread slices, Italian bread
- 2 tbsp. melted butter

Directions:

1. Preheat the sandwich maker.
2. In a bowl combine the sugar and cream cheese. Blend until soft. Add the chocolate and bananas, mix again.
3. Spread on 4 Italian bread slices and cover with the other bread slices.
4. Brush sides with butter.
5. Grill for about 2 minutes.
6. Cut the sandwiches in half and serve.

Zucchini parmesan sandwich grill

Prep Time/Cook Time: 10 Minutes, Serves: 2 Sandwiches

Ingredients:

- 4 slices whole-wheat bread
- ½ tsp olive oil
- 1 medium zucchini, sliced lengthwise
- ¼ cup fresh basil leaves
- 2 tbsps. balsamic vinegar
- 1 tsp Parmesan cheese, grated

Directions:

1. Lightly pat olive oil on each sandwich maker pan.

2. Glaze the zucchini and one side of each bread with balsamic vinegar.

3. Make sandwiches, layering the zucchini, basil leaves, and Parmesan.

4. Cook in sandwich maker for about 5 minutes.

5. Serve hot.

Quick & Easy Egg Muffin Sandwiches

Prep Time/Cook Time: 15 Minutes, Serves: 1

Ingredients:

- 1 whole-wheat English muffin (split & toasted)
- 1 egg
- 1 tsp. water
- 2 tbsps. shredded cheese
- Salt & pepper (to taste)
- 1 tbsp. mayonnaise
- ½ tsp. Dijon mustard

Directions:

1. Break an egg into a microwave-safe pot; add water & beat until well combined.
2. Then, sprinkle cheese on the top of the egg mixture and place in microwave.
3. Next, cook for about 35 to 40 seconds or until all the liquid is evaporated.
4. In the meanwhile; spread the mayonnaise on each half of English muffin with Dijon mustard on one side.
5. Once, the egg is set, place it on top of bread & with other half of the bread.

Grilled spaghetti bites

Prep Time/Cook Time: 45 Minutes, Serves: 2

Ingredients:

- 4 slices whole-wheat bread
- ½ tsp olive oil
- ½ cup spaghetti, cooked or leftover
- 8 strips extra-lean turkey bacon, defrosted
- 1 tbsp. Parmesan cheese, grated (optional)

Directions:

1. Lightly pat oil on each sandwich maker pan.
2. Place two bread slices on the sandwich maker.
3. Top with spaghetti and cheese.
4. Top with the two remaining bread slices.
5. Cook in sandwich maker for about 3 minutes.
6. Serve hot.

Fluffy Sandwich

Prep Time/Cook Time: 15 Minutes, Serves: 2 Sandwiches

Ingredients

- 2 tbsps. peanut butter
- 2 slices bread
- 2 1/2 tbsps. marshmallow cream

Directions

1. Lay two pieces of bread flat on a working surface.

2. Coat one piece of bread with peanut butter, and another piece with marshmallow cream.

3. Now microwave the pieces of bread for 30 secs with the highest power setting.

4. Form the pieces into a sandwich and enjoy with milk.

Aloha pizza-wich

Prep Time/Cook Time: 10 Minutes, Serves: 2 sandwiches

Ingredients:

- 2 whole-wheat tortillas
- ½ tsp olive oil
- 2 slices extra lean ham
- 2 slices canned unsweetened pineapple rings
- ½ cup part-skim mozzarella cheese, shredded
- 1 tsp dried herbs of choice (oregano, basil, rosemary, thyme, etc.)

Directions:

1. Lightly pat olive oil on each sandwich maker pan.
2. Make tortilla folds, layering each filling ingredient.
3. Cook in sandwich maker for about 5 minutes.
4. Serve hot.

Onion Bread Blueprint for Sandwiches

Prep Time/Cook Time: 45 Minutes, Serves: 12 Sandwiches

Ingredients

- ¾ c. / 200 ml lukewarm milk

- 5 tbsps. lukewarm water

- 3 tbsps. butter, softened

- 1 ½ tsps. salt

- 3 tbsps. white sugar

- 1 tsp onion powder

- 3 tbsps. dried minced onion

- ¼ c / 50 g instant potato flakes

- 3 c. / 390 g all-purpose flour

- 1 (.25 oz. / 8 g) envelope active dry yeast

- 1 egg white

- 1 tbsp. water

- ¼ c. / 30 g dried minced onion

Directions

1. Add the following to a bread machine and set the machine to the dough cycle: yeast, milk, flour, water, potato flakes, butter, 3 tablespoons of dried onions, salt, onion powder, and sugar.

2. Now work the dough on a cutting board coated with flour for 2 minutes then slice the dough into 8 pieces.

3. Shape each piece into a ball then flatten each one.

4.   Place the flattened dough in a jellyroll pan which has been coated with nonstick spray and place a kitchen towel over everything.

5.   Let the dough sit for 50 minutes.

6.   Now set your oven to 350 °F / 180°C before doing anything else.

7.   Get a small bowl and whisk your water and egg together. Top the rolls with the egg wash then coat each one with the rest of the minced onions.

8.   Cook everything in the oven for 17 minutes.

9.   Enjoy.

Pepperoni pizza-wich

Prep Time/Cook Time: 10 Minutes, Serves: 2

Ingredients:

- 2 tortillas
- 1 tsp olive oil
- 12 pepperoni slices
- ½ cup part-skim mozzarella cheese, shredded
- ¼ cup tomato paste
- 1 tsp dried herbs of choice (oregano, basil, rosemary, thyme, etc.)

Directions:

1. Lightly pat olive oil on each sandwich maker pan.
2. Lightly spread olive oil and then tomato paste on one side of each tortilla.
3. Make tortilla folds, layering the other ingredients.
4. Cook in sandwich maker for about 3 minutes.
5. Serve hot.

Toasted Cinnamon Sandwich

Prep Time/Cook Time: 20 Minutes, Serves: 3

Ingredients

- 2 links pork sausage links
- 1 slice Cheddar cheese
- 2 frozen waffles, toasted
- ¼ Red Delicious apple, sliced very thin
- ½ tsp cinnamon-sugar

Directions

1. Stir fry your sausage for 6 minutes until it is fully done.
2. Lay one piece of cheese on a waffle then place your apples on top of the cheese.
3. Top the apples with the cinnamon-sugar and the sausage.
4. Place the apples over the waffles and slice the sandwich in half.
5. Enjoy.

Cheesy bacon grill

Prep Time/Cook Time: 15 Minutes, Serves: 2

Ingredients:

- 4 slices whole-wheat bread
- ½ tsp light butter
- 8 strips extra-lean turkey bacon
- ¼ cup onions, chopped
- ½ cup part-skim mozzarella cheese, shredded

Directions:

1. Lightly pat butter on each sandwich maker pan.
2. Make two sandwiches, layering the turkey bacon, cheese, and onions.
3. Cook in sandwich maker for about 5 minutes.
4. Serve hot.

Cheesy broccoli sandwich

Prep Time/Cook Time: 10 Minutes, Serves: 2 Sandwiches

Ingredients:

- 4 slices whole-wheat bread
- ½ tsp light butter
- ½ cup broccoli flowers, sliced
- ½ cup reduced-fat cheddar cheese, shredded

Directions:

1. Lightly pat butter on each sandwich maker pan.
2. Make two sandwiches, layering the broccoli and cheese.
3. Cook in sandwich maker for about 3-5 minutes.
4. Serve hot.

Sandwich on a Stick

Prep Time/Cook Time: 20 Minutes, Serves: 4 Sandwiches

Ingredients

- 8 (6-inch) skewers
- 4 oz. deli sliced lemon chicken or smoked turkey breast
- 1 cup chopped arugula
- 4 oz. Colby jack cheese, cut into small squares
- 1 cup grape tomatoes
- ½ cup small dill pickles
- ¾ cup ranch dressing or deli mustard (optional)

Directions:

1. Saturate skewers in water for half an hour.
2. Thread skewers with chicken (or turkey) arugula, cheese, tomatoes and pickles.
3. Serve up with ranch dressing or mustard for dipping.

Sweet Potato and Avocado Sandwich

Prep Time/Cook Time: 30 Minutes, Serves: 2 Sandwiches

Ingredients

- Sweet potatoes
- Olive oil
- Sea Salt
- Avocado
- Red pepper (you can use fresh or roasted, both are good just different flavors)
- Black Bean Hummus

Directions:

1. Pre-heat the oven to 425 F.
2. Slice sweet potatoes into rounds.
3. Drizzle or spray the sweet potato rounds with olive oil then sprinkle with salt.
4. Roast for approximately about 20 minutes.
5. Pull out of the oven and cool.
6. When cool spread the sweet potatoes with black bean spread.
7. Apply the sliced avocado, and sliced red pepper to the sandwich.
8. Add atop with the sweet potato round.

Paleo Mushroom and Bacon Sandwich

Prep Time/Cook Time: 45 Minutes, Serves: 12 Sandwiches

Ingredients:

- 2 portabella caps with stems removed
- 1 tablespoon olive oil
- 3 slices bacon (turkey or ham)
- 2 slices tomato
- 1/8 teaspoon fresh ground pepper
- ½ cup spinach
- ½ avocado

Directions:

1. Wash mushroom caps and scoop out gills.Mix the pepper with the olive oil.
2. Place mushrooms gill side down into the mixture.
3. On a heated grill, grill mushrooms for 3- 5 minutes or until they start to brown. Remove from heat.
4. To assemble your sandwich; top one mushroom with the bacon, tomatoes and spinach, sliced avocado and sprinkle some of the remaining oil and pepper mixture unto the filling.
5. Combine with the other mushroom, cut into halves or bite in whole.
6. Enjoy!

Buffalo Chicken Sandwiches

Prep Time/Cook Time: 45 Minutes, Serves: 14

Ingredients

- 3 large eggs
- 1 cup almond butter or cashew butter, (250 mL)
- ¼ cup extra virgin coconut oil raw, (60 mL)
- 1 tsp cream of tartar, (5 mL)
- ½ tsp baking soda, (2 mL)
- 1/8 tsp salt, (0.5 mL)
- Sesame seeds for decoration
- 1 egg white to brush on the buns

Directions:

1. Pre-heat stove to 350°F.
2. Line a baking sheet with parchment paper.
3. In a dish, mix together the eggs and cream of tartar.
4. Blend until whipped and frothy.
5. Place in the almond butter, coconut oil.
6. Finally add baking soda and salt and blend until smooth.
7. Spoon the batter onto the sheet so it creates individual mini buns, 1-1 .5" wide.
8. Brush egg whites on every bun.
9. Sprinkle sesame seeds on the buns.
10. Cook for 12 minutes or until a tooth pick can be applied and come out nice and clean.

Paleo Eggs & Tomato Sandwich

Prep Time/Cook Time: 20 Minutes, Serves: 3

Ingredients:

- 2 eggs
- 2 large tomatoes
- 1 tablespoon olive oil
- ¼ cup sliced mushrooms
- A dash of salt and pepper to taste

Directions:

1. Horizontally, cut the tomatoes in half and carefully remove the seeds and some of the seed membrane, depending on how much filling you have. Then set aside.
2. In a bowl beat the eggs, adding the salt and pepper. Then set aside.
3. In a medium skillet heat the oil over medium heat, you can cut the mushrooms into smaller pieces or leave them as they are, then add them. Cook the mushrooms until they are tender.
4. Pour the egg mixture into the skillet and then let it sit for about 15 seconds.
5. Then fold over the eggs from the bottom of the pan with a wooden spoon, let them sit again, then stir again.Let it be a soft set.
6. To assemble the sandwich, spoon mixture into each half of the tomatoes and then combine.
7. This is best served warm. Enjoy!

Paleo Sweet potato Sandwich

Prep Time/Cook Time: 10 Minutes, Serves: 2 Sandwiches

Ingredients:

- 2 slices of cooked purple sweet potato
- 4 Tablespoons coconut oil
- 2 slices of tomatoes
- 3 slices cooked bacon

- Scrambled eggs (softly set)
- A dash of fresh ground pepper
- 1/8 teaspoon cumin
- ½ teaspoon garlic powder
- A dash of salt

Directions:

1. In a large skillet, heat 3 tablespoons of the coconut oil. Combine spices, salt and 1 tablespoon of the coconut oil, mix well.
2. Coat the potato slices with the spice mixture and lightly fry over medium heat for 5 minutes or until slightly brown on each side. Use a wide metal spatula to flip the potatoes to prevent it from breaking.
3. Let the potatoes cool before assembling the sandwich.
4. Assemble the sandwich by topping a potato slice with the scrambled eggs and bacon, topping with the tomatoes then the other slice of the sweet potato.
5. Enjoy!

Paleo Bell pepper Sandwich

Prep Time/Cook Time: 15 Minutes, Serves: 3 Sandwiches

Ingredients:

- 3 thin slices of ham
- 1 large red bell pepper
- ½ avocado (sliced

Directions:

1. To assemble your sandwich; cut the bell pepper in half, sideways and remove the seeds and seed membrane.

2. Then just add your filling, which in this recipe are your ham and avocado slices, stuffing them between the two halves of the bell pepper.

3. Enjoy!

Portabella and Halloumi Burger

Prep Time/Cook Time: 45 Minutes, Serves: 2 Sandwiches

Ingredients

- 4 portabella mushroom caps with stems removed
- 2 tbsps. olive oil
- 3 ½ tbsps. balsamic vinegar
- 2 slices tomato
- 2 slices halloumi
- ½ cup basil leaves
- ¼ tsp pepper
- ¼ tsp sea salt

Directions

1. Warm grill to medium-high temperature.
2. Wash the mushroom caps and then dry.
3. In a container, blend balsamic vinegar and olive oil.
4. Position the mushrooms gill side down in the mix.
5. Grill the mushrooms on the gill side first for approximately 5 minutes or till they begin to sweat.
6. Flip over, grill 2 to 3 minutes more.
7. Position the halloumi on grill and grill 2 minutes on both sides over fairly high heat.
8. Add salt and pepper onto the tomato.
9. Assemble the "burger", mushroom as the bun, the halloumi cheese as the burger, add mildly salted tomato and crisp basil leaves.
10. Wrap up and serve.

Paleo Tuna Cucumber Sandwich

Prep Time/Cook Time: 15 Minutes, Serves: 2 Sandwiches

Ingredients:

- 1 can drained tuna packed in water
- 1 cucumber
- ½ avocado
- 1 teaspoon of olive oil (optional)
- A dash of salt and pepper to taste

Directions:

1. Cut the cucumber half and remove the seeds and some of the membrane, depending on how much filling you have.
2. Mix the membrane with the tuna, salt pepper and oil.
3. Pour mixture into one of the halved cucumbers, then combined the other half to form a sandwich.
4. Enjoy!

White chocolate macadamia nut sandwich

Prep Time/Cook Time: 15 Minutes, Serves: 2

Ingredients:

- ¼ cup roasted macadamia nuts, chopped
- 6 squares white chocolate, crushed
- 4 slices whole-wheat bread
- ½ tsp light butter

Directions:

1. Lightly pat butter on each sandwich maker pan.
2. Make two sandwiches with sprinkles of macadamia chops and white chocolate bits.
3. Cook in sandwich maker for about 3 minutes.
4. Serve hot.

CHAPTER 11: A 30-DAY MEAL PLAN

Day 1:
Breakfast: Cheese and Egg Sandwich
Lunch: Guacamole sandwich grill
Dinner: Cherry Chocolate Sandwich

Day 2:
Breakfast: Toasted Cinnamon Sandwich
Lunch: Fluffy Sandwich
Dinner: Cheesy bacon grill

Day 3:
Breakfast: Corned Beef and Sauerkraut Sandwich
Lunch: Apricot Chicken Sandwich
Dinner: Tuna and Lettuce Sandwich

Day 4:
Breakfast: Breakfast Hamburger
Lunch: Buffalo Chicken Grilled Cheese Sandwich
Dinner: Crab Salad Sandwich

Day 5:
Breakfast: Bacon Hawaiian Sandwich
Lunch: Easy Ginger Beef Sandwiches
Dinner: Gourmet Chicken and Mushroom Sandwich

Day 6:
Breakfast: Vegetarian Omelet Sandwich

Lunch: Turkey Club
Dinner: Italian Meatball Sub

Day 7:
Breakfast: Traditional BLT
Lunch: Sausage and Cheese
Dinner: Baked Turkey Sandwich

Day 8:
Breakfast: Steak Sandwiches
Lunch: Pepperoni pizza-wich
Dinner: Paleo Bell pepper Sandwich

Day 8:
Breakfast: Mediterranean Sandwiches
Lunch: Classic Egg, Ham and Cheese
Dinner: French Toast Sandwich

Day 9:
Breakfast: Roast Beef and Provolone Sandwich
Lunch: Grilled Chicken & Apple Sandwiches
Dinner: Turkey Club

Day 10:
Breakfast: Cheese and Egg Sandwich
Lunch: Chicken Hot and Sour Sandwich
Dinner: Hot Seafood Sandwiches

Day 11:
Breakfast: French Toast Sandwich
Lunch: Turkey Club

Dinner: Mediterranean
Sandwiches

Day 12:
Breakfast: Avocado, Swiss and
Bacon
Lunch:
Dinner:

Day 13:
Breakfast: Spinach, Parmesan and
Egg White
Lunch: Turkey corned beef and
cabbage sandwich
Dinner: Mediterranean
Sandwiches

Day 14:
Breakfast: Salmon and cream
cheese grilled sandwich
Lunch: Nutella Sandwich
Dinner: Peanut Butter Bagel
Sandwich

Day 15:
Breakfast: Cheesy broccoli
sandwich
Lunch: Apricot Chicken Sandwich
Dinner: Microwave Tuna
Sandwiches

Day 16:
Breakfast: Turkey corned beef
and cabbage sandwich
Lunch: Mediterranean
Sandwiches
Dinner: Italian Meatball Sub

Day 17:

Breakfast: Buffalo Chicken
Sandwiches
Lunch: Traditional BLT
Dinner: Grilled hummus sandwich

Day 18:
Breakfast: Sausage and Cheese
Lunch: Asian bean sprouts salad-
wich
Dinner: Caramel Strawberries
Sandwich

Day 19:
Breakfast: Grilled spaghetti bites
Lunch: Paleo Sweet potato
Sandwich
Dinner: Apricot Chicken Sandwich

Day 20:
Breakfast: Easy Ginger Beef
Sandwiches
Lunch: Grilled Chicken & Apple
Sandwiches
Dinner: Grilled hummus sandwich

Day 21:
Breakfast: Caramel Strawberries
Sandwich
Lunch: Buffalo Chicken
Sandwiches
Dinner: Aloha pizza-wich

Day 22:
Breakfast: Bacon Hawaiian
Sandwich
Lunch: Baked Turkey Sandwich
Dinner: Guacamole sandwich grill

Day 23:

Breakfast: Cheesy broccoli
sandwich
Lunch: Paleo Eggs & Tomato
Sandwich
Dinner: Vegetarian Omelet
Sandwich

Day 24:
Breakfast: Sweet Potato Cakes
Burger
Lunch: Italian Meatball Sub
Dinner: Buffalo Chicken
Sandwiches

Day 25:
Breakfast: Chicken Hot and Sour
Sandwich
Lunch: Eggs Florentine Biscuit
Dinner: Apricot Chicken Sandwich

Day 26:
Breakfast: Vegetarian Patty
Sandwich
Lunch: Guacamole sandwich grill
Dinner: Buffalo Chicken
Sandwiches

Day 27:

Breakfast: Baked Turkey
Sandwich
Lunch: The Rustic Beef Sandwich
Dinner: Deli Corned Beef Slaw
Sandwiches

Day 28:
Breakfast: Breakfast Hamburger
Lunch: Wasabi mayo shrimp
sandwich
Dinner: Italian Meatball Sub

Day 29:
Breakfast: Apple cinnamon
sandwich
Lunch: Buffalo Chicken
Sandwiches
Dinner: French Toast Sandwich

Day 30:
Breakfast: Grilled Chicken &
Apple Sandwiches
Lunch: Beef and Mushroom
Sandwich
Dinner: Easy Ginger Beef
Sandwiches

APPENDIX : RECIPES INDEX

Peanut Butter Bagel Sandwich 80
Pepperoni pizza-wich 92
Pork Rib Sandwich 25
Portabella and Halloumi Burger 103
Portabella and Halloumi Burger 72
Prosciutto and Provolone Sandwich 74

Q

Quick & Easy Egg Muffin Sandwiches 86

R

Raspberry Sandwich 83
Roast Beef and Provolone Sandwich 32
Roast Beef Sandwiches 21

S

Salmon and cream cheese grilled
sandwich 47
Sandwich on a Stick 96
Sausage and Cheese 17
Scrambled Egg and Easy Ham Sandwich
19
Spanish sardines sandwich 46
Spinach, Parmesan and Egg White 12
Steak Sandwiches 66
Sweet Potato and Avocado Sandwich 97
Sweet Potato Cakes Burger 64

T

The Rustic Beef Sandwich 26
Toasted Cinnamon Sandwich 93
Traditional BLT 10
Tuna and Lettuce Sandwich 50
Tuna nicoise salad-wich 45
Turkey Burgers 68
Turkey Club 71
Turkey corned beef and cabbage
sandwich 37

V

Vegan Sausage Sandwich 57
Vegetarian Omelet Sandwich 61
Vegetarian Patty Sandwich 59

W

Waffle, Egg and Sausage 16
Warm California maki sandwich 48
Wasabi mayo shrimp sandwich 52
White chocolate macadamia nut
sandwich 105

Z

Zucchini parmesan sandwich grill 85

Printed by Libri Plureos GmbH in Hamburg,
Germany